Contents

Some words are printed in bold, **like this**. You can find out what they mean in the glossary. You can also look in the box at the bottom of the page where the word first appears.

GREAT ADVENTURERS

Some people enjoy the comforts of home. Others choose to go places they know will be uncomfortable, and even dangerous.

Great firsts

Adventurers in the 1900s endangered their lives to be the first to reach different places. People travelled at great risk and expense to the North and South poles. Others scaled Earth's highest mountains. Some even went to the Moon.

Thanks to earlier explorers, today we know what the world looks like in great detail.

frontier   area on the edge of settled parts of a country

ATOMIC

GREAT ADVENTURERS

ANN WEIL

Raintree

www.raintreepublishers.co.uk
Visit our website to find out more information about **Raintree** books.

To order:
 Phone 44 (0) 1865 888112
 Send a fax to 44 (0) 1865 314091
Visit the Raintree bookshop at **www.raintreepublishers.co.uk** to browse our catalogue and order online.

First published in Great Britain by
Raintree, Halley Court, Jordan Hill,
Oxford OX2 8EJ, part of Harcourt
Education. Raintree is a registered
trademark of Harcourt Education Ltd.

© Harcourt Education Ltd 2007
First published in paperback in 2007.
The moral right of the proprietor has been asserted.

Editorial: Louise Galpine, Rosie Gordon,
Dave Harris, and Stig Vatland
Design: Victoria Bevan and Bigtop
Picture Research: Hannah Taylor and Sally Clakton
Production: Camilla Crask

Originated by Chroma Graphics Pte. Ltd
Printed and bound in China by WKT

10 digit ISBN 1 406 20354 8 (hardback)
13 digit IBSN 978 1 406 20354 7
11 10 09 08 07
10 9 8 7 6 5 4 3 2 1

10 digit ISBN 1 406 20375 0 (paperback)
13 digit IBSN 978 1 406 20375 2
12 11 10 09 08
10 9 8 7 6 5 4 3 2 1

British Library Cataloguing in Publication Data
Weil, Ann
Great Adventurers. – (Atomic)
910.9'22
A full catalogue record for this book is available
from the British Library.

Acknowledgements
The author and publisher are grateful to the
following for permission to reproduce copyright
material: Alamy Images, pp. **4–5** (Dave Willis/
Sylvia Cordaiy Photo Library Ltd), **8–9**, (Royal
Geographical Society/George Band); Bruce Kirkby,
pp. **22–23**; Corbis, p. **25**; Corbis, pp. **16–17**,
18–19 (Royalty Free), **12–13**, **14–15**, **15**,
(Bettmann), **18-19** (Sygma), **10-11** (Paul A
Souders), **20–21** (Ralph White), **26** bot (Reuters);
Empics pp. **6**, (AP/ Diane Bondareff), **20** (AP/Mike
Kullen); Getty Images pp. **28–29** (Photodisc);
yourexpedition.com, p. **26** top.
Cover: Getty Images/ New York Times Co.

The publishers would like to thank Diana Bentley,
Nancy Harris, and Dee Reid for their assistance in the
preparation of this book.

Every effort has been made to contact copyright holders
of any material reproduced in this book. Any omissions
will be rectified in subsequent printings if notice is given
to the publishers.

Adventurers today still take risks, but they use the best equipment to help them survive their adventures.

Adventurous fact!

Daniel Boone explored parts of the U.S. frontier in the 1700s and 1800s. He bragged, "I have never been lost, but I will admit to being confused for several weeks."

MacArthur set the record sailing a 23-metre (75-foot) trimaran.

Adventurous fact!

Canadian adventurer Joshua Slocum sailed around the world solo in the late 1800s. It took him three years.

AROUND THE WORLD IN A SAILING BOAT

"It has been an unbelievable journey," said 28-year-old Ellen MacArthur when she set a record time for sailing around the world solo.

Adventure at sea

In 2005 the British sailor braved huge waves and strong winds, dodged icebergs, and almost hit a whale. She finished her 34,500–kilometre (27,000–mile) trip in less than 72 days. "I always believed I could break the record," she said, "but I really didn't think I would do it at the first attempt."

Still, winning isn't everything. "Learning," MacArthur said. "That's what's important. Learning and challenging myself."

solo	alone; by yourself
trimaran	fast sailing boat with three main bodies, or hulls

CLIMBING TO THE TOP OF THE WORLD

In 1953 Edmund Hillary from New Zealand and Tenzing Norgay from Tibet became the first people to stand on the top of Mount Everest.

Almost crushed by ice!

As they descended Hillary stepped on a large chunk of ice stuck on an ice wall. The chunk came loose, causing Hillary to fall down a **crevasse**. Hillary said, "I realized, if I wasn't careful, I'd be crushed between the ice and the wall of the crevasse." Luckily, Tenzing acted quickly. He caught Hillary's rope and stopped him falling to an icy death.

Adventurous fact!

Mount Everest is on the border of Nepal and Tibet. Its summit is the highest place on Earth, at 8,850 metres (29,035 feet) above sea level.

border — imaginary line that separates two countries

crevasse — large, deep crack in the ice

CHINA

TIBET

NEPAL   Mt. Everest

N
W   E
S

INDIA

INDIAN
OCEAN

Hillary and Tenzing
had a cold, dangerous
adventure.

sea level   level of the ocean, used as
a starting point for measuring
the height of mountains and
other natural features

summit   top or highest point

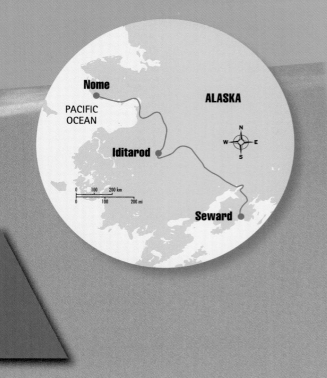

Nome

PACIFIC OCEAN

ALASKA

N
W E
S

Iditarod

0   100   200 km
0   100   200 mi

Seward

Butcher races through miles of icy wasteland.

Braving Alaska

In the 1980s and 1990s, U.S. adventurer Susan Butcher won the Iditarod four times. This famous race is held annually in Alaska.

Moose attack!

People called **mushers** drive teams of twelve to sixteen sled dogs from Anchorage to Nome, over more than 1,600 kilometres (1,000 miles) of wilderness.

During one race, Butcher and her dogs were attacked by a moose. The moose killed two of her dogs.

A freezing fall

Another time, Butcher and her sled fell through the ice into the freezing water below. The dogs valiantly pulled her and the sled out onto solid ice. Butcher was drenched and freezing cold, but alive.

annually	**once every year**
musher	**person who drives a dogsled**

A Plane Disappears

In 1932 U.S. pilot Amelia Earhart became the first woman to fly a plane across the Atlantic Ocean **solo**.

Lost at sea?

In 1937 Earhart and Fred Noonan attempted an around-the-world flight. Unfortunately, they never made it. A ship waiting near a refuelling stop received a message: "We must be on you [on target] but cannot see you . . . fuel is running low." Half an hour later, Earhart sent one last message stating her position.

People searched for their plane, but found nothing. Most people assumed Earhart and Noonan died when they crashed into the ocean, but their disappearance is still a mystery.

Adventurous fact!

Earhart was pictured on a U.S. postage stamp in 1963.

Earhart is one of the most famous pilots in history.

Adventurous fact!

Hughes flew from New York to Paris in a record-breaking 16 hours and 38 minutes. Today planes are much faster.

Hughes designed his own aircraft. Many of his ideas are still used today.

FASTEST FLIGHT AROUND THE WORLD

Howard Hughes was famous in the United States for being incredibly rich. In 1938 he took off on a daring around-the-world flight.

Flying against the wind

Hughes wanted to set a new speed record. But there was a strong wind. As he sped toward Paris, France, the plane required more fuel to keep up its speed. "I hope we get to Paris before we run out of fuel", Hughes radioed from his plane over the Atlantic Ocean. Luckily, Hughes made it to Paris and refuelled, before achieving his round–the–world record.

Howard Hughes was greeted by crowds in Los Angeles when he completed his record-breaking world trip.

MOUNTAIN MAN

In the early 1800s, adventurous Americans trapped beavers for the fur trade. They were called mountain men.

Path finder

The most famous mountain man was Jedediah Smith. He guided a group of mountain men into the dangerous Rocky Mountains. He found the **South Pass**, which was later used by settlers when they moved west to Oregon and California.

Bear attack!

One time a grizzly bear fiercely attacked Smith. It crushed his ribs and ripped off his **scalp** with its long, sharp claws. Smith survived the bear attack, but his scalp was precariously hanging off the side of his head. Another mountain man sewed it back on.

Adventurous fact!

After the bear attack, Smith wore long hair to hide his scar and missing eyebrow.

An adult grizzly bear is 1.8–2.5 metres (6–8 feet) long.

fur trade	trade in skins of animals trapped in North America in the 1800s
scalp	skin and hair on top of a person's head
South Pass	way through the Rocky Mountains

Collins has said, "We fly knowing that there's risk."

Adventurous fact!

Collins commanded her first space mission in 1999.

Shuttle Commander

On 26 July, 2005, **space shuttle** *Discovery* lifted off with U.S. astronaut Eileen Collins in command. This was the first shuttle **mission** since *Columbia* crashed in 2003, killing all seven astronauts on board.

Would disaster strike again?

A piece of foam detached and flew off as *Discovery* lifted off. This was the same thing that had happened to *Columbia* before it crashed. For fourteen days, people watched, waited, and feared the same tragic ending might happen again.

But this time, the space shuttle returned safely to Earth. It was another successful mission for Eileen Collins.

mission job or assignment

space shuttle spacecraft that takes off like a rocket and lands like an aeroplane

FINDING TITANIC

U.S. scientist Robert Ballard found the shipwreck *Titanic* in 1985. The *Titanic* sank in 1912, after hitting an iceberg.

Underwater and outer space

Locating the shipwreck took many years. The **ocean floor** is mostly unknown. Exploring it is like exploring outer space. In the depths of the ocean it is pitch dark and very cold, and the **pressure** of the water on a person's body can be deadly.

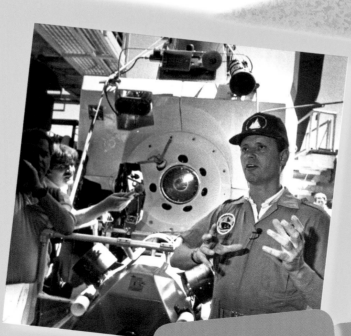

Ballard helped invent a new way to see the ocean floor, using robot submarines with cameras.

dissolve   spread throughout a liquid

ocean floor   bottom of the ocean

A robot took this picture of the wreck of *Titanic*, 3.2 kilometres (2 miles) deep under water.

Adventurous fact!

About 1,500 people died when *Titanic* sank. A student asked whether Ballard found skeletons. Ballard explained that bones dissolve in the ocean. Only the passengers' shoes were left.

pressure   when a force is pushed against something else

shipwreck   sunken ship

A boat such as this does not offer much protection from the dangers of the Blue Nile.

WILD RIVER

A huge crocodile rises from the black surface of the water. There is a hissing sound as its jaws open wide...

Croc attack!

Canadian adventurer Bruce Kirkby was on a rafting trip on the Blue Nile River in Africa when a crocodile attacked.

No-one on the rafting trip had a gun to scare off the crocodile. Instead, they threw stones at the huge beast. Luckily for them, the crocodile surrendered and swam away.

Adventurous fact!

Kirkby knew this trip was risky. Even more dangerous than crocodiles were bandits who robbed and killed people for their belongings. Adventurers on an earlier trip were murdered.

bandit   robber

RACE TO THE SOUTH POLE

In 1911 Norwegian explorer Roald Amundsen became the first person to reach the South Pole.

From the ice to the air

Amundsen used **dog sleds** to win a race to the South Pole against British explorer Robert Scott. After that success, Amundsen took to the air. In 1926 he flew over the North Pole in a **blimp**. Two years later, he died in a plane crash on a rescue mission to help another explorer, whose plane had gone down near the North Pole.

Adventurous fact!

In 1912 Robert Scott was the second person to reach the South Pole. He and the four men with him froze to death on their way back.

blimp	airship filled with gas, like a balloon
dog sled	sled pulled by dogs

Amundsen once said, "Adventure is just bad planning."

Three million students in 65 countries used the Internet to follow Bancroft and Arnesen's progress.

TODAY'S POLAR EXPLORERS

In 2000 Liv Arnesen from Norway and Ann Bancroft from the United States began to cross the frozen continent of Antarctica. One day the wind was howling, so Bancroft did not hear the crash as Arnesen fell through a crack in the ice.

A very close call

After Arnesen crawled out of the ice, she realized Bancroft was on the edge of a **crevasse** herself. They had come very close to disaster. "Suddenly, I just started laughing," Arnesen said. "I was grateful to be alive."

Despite this ordeal the two women went on to finish their journey.

Adventurous fact!

Bancroft and Arnesen used skis and sails to pull their sleds across Antarctica.

ADVENTURERS TODAY AND TOMORROW

The highest mountains have been climbed. The North and South Poles have been explored. People have gone around the world by boat, plane, and spacecraft. There are not many "firsts" left to do.

A need to explore

Still, even today adventurers with imagination and courage are going to new places and discovering new ways to get there.

"I am a huge believer in human exploration," astronaut Eileen Collins said. "I think we humans have something inside us, a need to explore. And I think some people have it more than others."

Are you an adventurer? Where would you like to explore?

A view of Earth from space
is something only a few
astronauts get to see.

Glossary

annually once every year

bandit robber

beaver furry animal with strong teeth, webbed feet, and a big, flat tail

blimp airship filled with gas, like a balloon

border imaginary line that separates two countries

crevasse large, deep crack in the ice

dissolve spread throughout a liquid

dog sled sled pulled by dogs

frontier area on the edge of settled parts of a country

fur trade trade in skins of animals trapped in North America in the 1800s

mission job or assignment

moose large forest animal with antlers

musher person who drives a dog sled

ocean floor bottom of the ocean

pressure when a force is pushed against something else

scalp skin and hair on top of a person's head

sea level level of the ocean, used as a starting point for measuring the height of mountains and other natural features

shipwreck sunken ship

solo alone; by yourself

South Pass way through the Rocky Mountains

space shuttle spacecraft that takes off like a rocket and lands like an aeroplane

summit top or highest point

trimaran fast sailing boat with three bodies, or hulls

Want to Know More?

Books

✳ *How High Can We Climb? The Story of Women Explorers*, Jeannine Atkins (Farrar, Straus, and Giroux, 2005)

✳ *The Encyclopedia of Explorers and Adventurers*, Justine Ciovacco (Franklin Watts, 2003)

✳ *Great Discoveries & Amazing Adventures*, Claire Llewellyn (Kingfisher, 2004)

Websites

✳ www.enchantedlearning.com/explorers
Find details of space, sea, and land explorers through the centuries.

✳ www.explorersweb.com
Get updates on recent adventures and tips on survival.

✳ http://kids.nasa.gov
The National Aeronautics and Space Administration website is all about space exploration.

If you liked this Atomic book, why don't you try these...?

Index

Notes for adults
Use the following questions to guide children towards identifying features of recount text:
Can you give examples of past tense language on page 8?
Can you find a recount of events on page 15?
Can you give an example of scene setting from page 19?
Can you find an example of a temporal connective on page 27?
Can you give an example of a closing statement from page 28?